MICHAEL DAUGHERTY
ASCLEPIUS
(2007)
FANFARE FOR BRASS AND PERCUSSION

HENDON MUSIC

BOOSEY & HAWKES

DISTRIBUTED BY

HAL•LEONARD®
CORPORATION
7777 W. BLUEMOUND RD. P.O. BOX 13819 MILWAUKEE, WI 53213

www.boosey.com
www.halleonard.com

Commissioned by Dr. Cyrus Farrehi
for the grand opening of the University of Michigan Cardiovascular Center

First performed on June 7, 2007 by the CVC Brass and Percussion Ensemble,
conducted by Emily Threinen

First recorded by the University of Michigan Symphony Band, conducted by Michael Haithcock,
on Equilibrium EQ86

BIOGRAPHY

Michael Daugherty is one of the most commissioned, performed and recorded living American composers on the concert music scene today. His music is rich with cultural and political allusions and bears the stamp of classic modernism, with colliding tonalities and blocks of sound; at the same time, his melodies can be eloquent and stirring. Hailed by *The Times* (London) as "a master icon maker" with a "maverick imagination, fearless structural sense and meticulous ear," Daugherty first came to international attention when his *Metropolis Symphony* was performed at Carnegie Hall in 1994 by the Baltimore Symphony Orchestra conducted by David Zinman.

Daugherty's works for wind ensemble and symphony band include *Desi* (1991), *Bizarro* (1993), *Motown Metal* (1994), *Niagara Falls* (1997), *Red Cape Tango* (1999), *UFO* (2000), *Rosa Parks Boulevard* (2001), *Bells for Stokowski* (2002), *Brooklyn Bridge* (2005), *Ladder to the Moon* (2006), *Raise the Roof* (2007), and *Asclepius* (2007).

Born in 1954 in Cedar Rapids, Iowa, Daugherty is the son of a dance-band drummer and the oldest of five brothers, all professional musicians. He studied music composition at the University of North Texas (1972-76), the Manhattan School of Music (1976-78) and computer music at Boulez's IRCAM in Paris (1979-80). Daugherty received his doctorate from Yale University in 1986 where his teachers included Jacob Druckman, Earle Brown, Roger Reynolds, and Bernard Rands. During this time, he also collaborated with jazz arranger Gil Evans in New York, and pursued further studies with composer György Ligeti in Hamburg, Germany (1982-84). After teaching music composition from 1986-1990 at the Oberlin Conservatory of Music, Daugherty joined the School of Music at the University of Michigan (Ann Arbor) in 1991, where he is Professor of Composition.

Daugherty has been the Composer-in-Residence with the Louisville Symphony Orchestra (2000), Detroit Symphony Orchestra (1999-2003), Colorado Symphony Orchestra (2001-02), Cabrillo Festival of Contemporary Music (2001-04, 2006-08), Westshore Symphony Orchestra (2005-06), Eugene Symphony (2006), the Henry Mancini Summer Institute (2006) and the Music from Angel Fire Chamber Music Festival (2006).

Daugherty has received numerous awards, distinctions and fellowships for his music; these include a Fulbright Fellowship (1977), the Kennedy Center Friedheim Award (1989) for his compositions *Snap!* and *Blue Like an Orange*, the Goddard Lieberson Fellowship from the American Academy of Arts and Letters (1991), fellowships from the National Endowment for the Arts (1992) and the Guggenheim Foundation (1996), and the Stoeger Prize from the Chamber Music Society of Lincoln Center (2000). In 2005, Daugherty received the Lancaster Symphony Orchestra Composer's Award, and in 2007, the Delaware Symphony Orchestra selected Daugherty as the winner of the A. I. duPont Award. Also in 2007, Daugherty was named "Outstanding Classical Composer" at the Detroit Music Awards and received the American Bandmasters Association Ostwald Award for his composition *Raise the Roof* for Timpani and Symphonic Band.

PROGRAM NOTE

Asclepius (2007) Fanfare for Brass and Percussion was commissioned by Dr. Cyrus Farrehi for the grand opening of the University of Michigan Cardiovascular Center. The work was premiered June 7, 2007 by the CVC Brass and Percussion Ensemble, conducted by Emily Threinen. The title refers to Asclepius [pronunciation: as-klee'-pee-uhs], the Greek God of medicine. Using the pulse of a beating heart as a musical metaphor, the majestic fanfare celebrates men and women who devote their lives to the noble cause of medical research and healing.

– Michael Daugherty

INSTRUMENTATION

4 F Horns

4 C Trumpets 1. Straight Metal Mute
                2. Straight Metal Mute
                3. Straight Metal Mute
                4. Straight Metal Mute

3 Trombones (3. Bass Trombone)
Tuba

Timpani (5 drums)
Percussion (2 players)
      1. Chimes, Suspended Cymbal, Crash Cymbals
      2. Glockenspiel, Metal (small anvil or brake drum)

Duration: ca. 5'30"

Score in C

SUGGESTED SEATING ARRANGEMENT

Percussion 1   Timpani   Percussion 2

Trumpet 4 3 2 1   Trombone 1 2 3   Tuba

Horn 4 3 2 1

Conductor

ASCLEPIUS

Fanfare for Brass and Percussion

Michael Daugherty
(2007)

979-0-051-66238-8

Printed in U.S.A.

12

24

L

molto rit.

N ♩ = 84, **Broadly**